# CAN OF WORMS

## THE SIEGE OF AN EMPYREAN

IRSHAD MUSHTAQ

# Contents

# Acknowledgements

With my deep sense of gratitude I would like to thank "The Almighty Allah" and then all those who made me more keen and enthusiastic through their precious words to put my ideas into this book.

I'm eternally grateful to my parents who took every step possible to make me an apt human being to perform in this complex modern world.They taught me the values of life and it's uncertainties. And played the role of a mentor in my life. Their hardwork and reliable efforts towards my life are the actual underpinning for me.

I also take this opportunity to express my gratitude to my friend Taha Tabish for helping me right along while writing this book. It's much harder to give your thoughts a shape of a book than it sounds. And without any support it's almost impossible.

And lastly, my thankfulness would be for the lovely readers. I would like to express my love to them for choosing my book with much of expectations and tenderness.

# Preface

As a child, fostered in a congenial breeze coming from the close mountains and streams of the crystal aqua particles. I had created the ambiance of my own. All I knew was the child inside me, my parents, friends and those orange sugar candies that made all my primary teeth look like broken black colored gates of calcium.

As I grew up and my basic senses matured, the perception of the world and life changed for me. The air filled with the smell of munition and I heard people talking about genocides and ethnic cleansing. My parents admitted me in the almamater, as I progressed in the classes, I started observing things and events that were way too agonizing.

As an amateur artist, I have tried to draw things rather than writing. I believe that the way you see the picture appeals to your emotions accordingly. This book "Can Of Worms" is the reflex of what I have been tapping eyes on. It gives unalloyed vista of Kashmir and it's folks. In the book are poems of harsh exactitude. Each verse or stanza has a life history and each word is the soul of the party.

# 1. Midnight December

In the freezing midnight of December enveloped
In a crystal white sheet of snow
Lives're chased by eyes in a 'casper'. Bow
To knees they ordered and curfewed

The city with a night raid not alien to city
They're there to perish one by one,
And sometimes massacred in million.
But a thing that has been nightmarish

And always unimagined is having to know
Which name is shortlisted for the role of convict
And who is to go through unseen script
Of ugly regime.

A script of an old father who sees
Hissen on the verge of despair
When his only bread earner in a deal unfair
Is seized without a record and pleas.

.

And on that night suspended of dreams
And dark of bounty, the misfortune assailed
Arshid and his family, when men prevailed

Over powerful resistant forces____forces,

.

Composed of a daughter whose guardian
Was being detained to practice his duty.
A disabled father wheelchaired of poverty,
For whom his son was the puller of cart

.

And a diabetic mother melting from age___
Oh! Why this cultured vale has unloosed it's chain
Of calm existence and now dwell in pain___
As they carried him off; from weak hands

.

Unironed, fell the 'Kangri' into disrepair
On the crystal white floor subdued
And amain turned the moisture unsubdued,
The ashes into black as if symbolising the darkness

Get going to rule the family, darkness, of a shadow
That whilom was counted with the body of their son,
And of silence of dried ocean
That was the only reserve of family.

# 2. Can Of Worms

Autumnal foliage bedazzle their orbs
When they keep walking on papers
Dyed scarlet brown, a calligraphy
Framed in the vital fluid of burghers.
Hail their geniuses

The gardens hue and cry, we will perish
In the haze of terror, that the guns roar
Ofttimes than the bulbul sings.
Fragrance of blood voyages every which way
Withal the peace dwells for aye in their published
Hail their geniuses

I see the Durgaras working in their ateliers
Sikhs spry in the towns On every split step
In high spirits, I see the snow lands of little Tibet
And then at 3 AM, a young is rescued
From his mother's dicey womb
The daybreakers of Kashmir so share the desire for peace
Hail their geniuses

What shall I say to show up
The can of worms when they come to see

My locale blooming with yemberzal, coucals say,
They, despite it ensue deaths, cast
It's name in the loveliest on earth.
Hail their geniuses

On the pillars of every sanctum
Ruined, gaudy gunshot wounds' art
Blessed with the tales of innocent terrorists
They try to harmonize it's wailing notes,
The blood with melted roses
The embers with bright cracker bonbons
Hail their geniuses

Flowers tolerate their own beauty now
Indifferently polished it's hue as well
Sentinels receive bouquet in white
While size varies diurnal from home
To home, and beyond the ideas
That skulk at liberty I say,
Hail their geniuses

# 3. Words Of Loss

Revel___Sepoy eclipse mankind in our land,
Did they In the knowledge-box of able fools___
With the spread of institutions of weaponry.

Eggplants loom in their reign in the role of the hand
Thrown small missiles___dust laden blood
Streams in slumber, slaying souls.

Lately O son, a long aged friend's words'___
Even when peace there's nothing to forget tho,
Traces were rubbed to the unreachable.

Now he sits locked inside my dome, not all there.
Fingertips don't portray him anymore
Nor the mouth, not about to

Doing so. Not are the fools the assassin
Rains pour where water is taken from
And mad we ask sun to behead the pourer.

.

Come not you my son, must not you as not you
Are to come here, now and forever.
As mad we as yet ask sun to behead the pourer.

Echoing inside, the hurricanes are but future
Quixotic perhaps, He and I and none...... and everyone
Cultivate, but not look into the eyes, son,

For executioner's awaiting the sun,
When red glow fills the sky and horizon
Appears that moonless night again.

They don't answer what's asked on roads
Crowded, crowded of carcasses and Pulwama
Thusly Vanished, so bid adieu to the City

And sing then___with fires___words of loss, at Chrar-e-Sharif( 1995)
In all new pangs, and then come back fistful.
Come back to question us, When did you die?

In those abrupt bazaars of Judas, a dissolved old nick
Or underneath a soldier's iron fastened shoes, melting
Rages for us. Long ago in Kashmir, how did you die?

# 4. Silences

Through ages suffering, deaths seldom nurse
Our doomsday, whilst transparent veil
Of Media pay a kindred spirit to autarch.
Not it blames crown as if would not fade
Ever. It blot out mirror from blind world
When we blot out mirror from blind us, Who's in the wrong.
We are a valley, which neither seem
To lack spring before springtime, for every morning

It seeds a new plant of mourning, nor appear
Perished, with the changing scenes of arts
And marts, Who's to blame. Such discipline with life
Art the nature by calm lonesomeness,
Lonesomeness as with the vouchsafement
Of curtains to the windowless. But yes we do resist,
Resist with a push button control, home-bound
Guarded of sweet potato scent, we execute

Our resistance, when a mosque colonnaded of cedars
Dissolve, before eyes, in the idiot box, only there.
As same as us, I too mount up a bluff of censure
Only in silence, amplifying my voice sitting next to wife
God must be proud of us, I think. As we maintain

Glorious death race naming immortality.
Passion presents gifts to fortune, but here
It's going around in circles, So the haven is in cage, but who's the gaoler.

# 5. Ahadis To Sepoy

Having buried in greed of beauties dense
Some left us thirsty in archaic market's debris

And of veil of humankind that fence
To safe, a deer and tiger with harmony

Stalwarts of early modern whom we mense
Made threads and hung with branches destiny.

Having buried in greed of independence
Some others caged us in asylum and called it impunity

And of water of Dal of our own, fragrance
They made to fade crimsoned stains gory

And those didn't disappear at broken edifice entrance
're glued at night with Sonmarg inhumanly.

Now what's left to rescind and whence
The floret are blazed in every village and city

And no more is discrete any nishat's stance
Not exclude a pasture poor everything cry out for liberty

# 6. Spiced Words Are Now The Eventide Silences

Brittle flowers of chinar, once reluctant to pardon
Our feet, are soaked now by years of privation.
Whispering, an old quill, the stories of childhood alleys
Are suffering the red ink only, from the nature in motley.
Brimming odour of tulips on beloved fields of pampore
Has put up a fetor-screen of belladonna.
But though every spiced word of pulchritude
In Rasul Mir's verses are turned to eventide silence,
Even if all beaming smiles through every window pane
Now are the frowns and grimaces of novel quixotes,
The dale's sun shall thrive and survive in our hearts

# 7. October 27

He annexed the stamps__looked for currency to breed__
With the ashes of peace, and rumoured
Of the arrivals that toil for the dreams of greed.

Separation__could be of no use__with these dire nights__
Did he announce__and mine becomes no power now
To give you the plume of your rights.

From every window pane vanished the views of emptiness
On the night of October 1947 in every street
When the military troops mighty and countless

Breathed our fate__thread bare__with the schnoz
Of their death instruments. And every lane institutionalized,
Darkened more and more, with the searchlights of our loss.

Yet no fear pleased our men to obey them but their greed
And desires of princely perfume, which made one
The unseemly Sheikh and other, the Abbas of misdeed.

Ever since the map__torn in two__occur only in newspapers
And ours is soaked too, in red ink, enveloped
With the__threads of euphony__confidence trick of armers.

Threads, but a noose that hangs us in oblivion
Nothing remains known in this sharp device and wise
We disclose everything and everything abandon.

# 8. Unwritten Streets

Without a lantern she was then and now
Holds no lamp, in the lanes echoing dark.
Do you hear Jhelum banks, beguile some time
Hoisting flags of dawn now,
In her dreams only.

She was the daughter of world yet blood
Soaked her beauty was then and now
Fenced of barbwire Leaves us in suspense,
If she ever was a beautiful bud
Or just a thorn flowerless.

Every hushed wave of Dal thirsty of water
Was then and now the country deluged with gore
As hearts row the boats of no concience
In the lake and barter
A life for a life.

.

Every street unwritten in Kalhana's time
Is rumored was destroyed by God himself.
Vanish your name___if you are satisfied___
From the list of sublime
And courageous' , says she.

And says, "my breath has been smoldering as cold
Winds jeweled of blood vapors of every son
Collide___since despots came___with Every thoroughfare
Of humankind. Yet I uphold
Holding my head high."

# 9. Poems Of Mehjoor And The Gupkar Threads

One night
A poor mother inherits
Dumb history, wrote with the dust
Of her son, sepulchered.

One night
Debauchery echos through
Every Jebel, where days
Of yore had martyrs' water
As a hosting memoir.

One night
The poems of Mehjoor
Are read clarion
On winter nights of
Each burgh.

One night
The patron of freedom,
Line zir pockets
By a thread of Gupkar.

One night
A warrior arms hissen
With minute pen to admit
Voice to the choked tongues.

One night
You and I, favoured of hell
Yet say farewell
To the revolution unconscientiously

# 10. Exodus? 90's Stratagem

You fled when hope was snuffed out
For one time in times, pitiless for you
I know, those wails you sent to me with a shout
Among the exploding lamps in dark blue
And your forever dissolved in rue.

But my each song has thousand words
Like you. Without a record of wooden panes,
Filthy and flocked of death birds,
Each mosque has undergone prayer refrains
Each shrine has soaked the blood stains.

I have thousand rivers water emptied,
Historical mosques turned to blaze
Of silence. Threshold of Jamia masjid
Is still waiting for muezzin, in large scales
Are cities unpacked and overcrowded are dark caves.

You left the bleeding Island sans taking in
Of whom the blood was. In the cold winds
Of terror, in every two there was a Muslim.
Ask them__when you die of age off hearts and minds
And trillions of lies__that who were blinds?

# 11. Discouraged Heaven

Are you in my hills
Resting in slopes of tenderness
Hiding under blankets of prettiness
Afraid of being killed

Are you in my orchards
Believing to bring in euphony
Restoring the discouraged heaven's glory
That could be seen in graveyards

Are you in the absence of ease in city
Besieged with injustice
Burning in the malice
Of soldiers fiercely

O dove of peace! Where are you
In this valley of turbulence
Are you alive anyplace
Unerringly will I ever see you.

# 12. "Firdaus"… Shallow Hopes

O Trader of peace! Shall my feet embark
On a human cry to reach you,
To hear your sigh of relief, shall all die
For only you devour the elegy of night.

My holy land is vandalised, aching my spirit
With it's ashes, terror winged is every page
Of memory. The image of home's shattered.

Childhood is nevermore a crowning jewel of life.
For children sway but on dead fathers' chest
Waving the flag of extremity and innocence.

Eternity in dry tears of sisters
Refuse to elapse a day.

Seasons of wrath certainly not drown
To reign, though every adoption of it has drowned.

.

.

.

O Trader of ataraxy! Could it be? You
Here again. To stop an eye to well up,
And break the silence of bulbul,
To name it again "Firdaus".

# 13. Poet Of Kashmir

Across the roads, draped
Of vast carpets of gore

Striding feet naked, send you cries
Countlessly, __be not irked__

Red painted insides of their eyelids
Spill drops of bane with their dreams

Of freedom, petrified deads
Warm tomorrow's bazaars of bulletin

For the world, and just yesterday
O! light of anything they want,

Srinagar was ploughed to soak
It's wettish soil sanguinary.

__Be not irked__ to raise the roof
Ecumenical, you speak little and more

You keep their hopes and dreams.
Be mehmood-esque, crucify with words

The usurper, be not irked by wails
Indite their woe and be the poet of Kashmir.

# 14. In Silence Is The Real Oppression

Her sightless eyes were “lately, I remember”
Flood channels, dry like September

With no tear yet drowning in perturbation
In search of letters from her dead son.

Dead in its eternity in the silences she own
She must see now in silence’s the real oppression

And most menacing is voicefullness for tyrant.
Her fussing hands mutilated imploring as vagrant

Longing for peace convinced that they pony up
She must think now of their spite and grow up

She must speak a little more to sharpen
The sun in us to breathe again for revolution.

# 15. My Poised Pen

Tear drenched papers gush the rains of blood
When my poised pen draw colors of those

Extrajudicial executions, that on each door
Have hanged empty memories of their lads

Memories of faces beautiful, in the azure peepers,
Which never blink in the angst to never see them again

And on the iced lips which're ready to emit not a word
In fear of losing the thirst of their names.

Words sprout__carrying the wounds of each pogrom__
From the pen, ever since they have cut my fingers

They hold weapon so do I, theirs' fire bullets of lie
Mine bestrew the ink of Mehmood's candor.

# 16. Stoicism Is Power

Beyond the mountains of this weakness
There lies a clime of intrepidness.
To reach there quest not for clime right,
Earn it with the power of this weakness.

You are not a demigod, rise not in a flash
Witness some days of struggle in lache
Sharpen your tool of hunger for release
Then shall you wing to sew whole your gash.

Do not spill drop by drop of jeremiad
As only in it has impossible defeat ever lied.
Meet hassles of solitaire everyday awelessly
Do not get the joy of release conspired.

In the gale shed leaves of your verve but remain
In the ruins, tarry a bit longer to regain
The contours of your moxie,
And arise as a warrior eternally insane.

.

.

.

Triumph goes to the strongest not always,
Nor should weaks Ever hold to be slaves
Burn not your meekness for aye, but when
The time is ripe leave the usurper in flames.

# 17. No Power Is Stable

Grieve not, lick no boot
For desert never pleads
In front of rain to shower.

It singes in it's dried blood
Like a lover who never received
It's love but feels the power

Of it's own. Beseech no foot
To stay with you, it's you adamant
To fend off the oppressor.

Let their sun scorch you brut
And no-rain salt your wounds,
Seek in every wound you suffer,

Liberation. Like the flowers hued,
Be not spooked of bees.
Shed fear of autumn's encounter

Of breeze and protrude
From the debris of incubus.
O brave heart of a warrior,

Grieve not, shoot
No words of Evanescence
For no power is stable in human matter.

# 18. The Pen Is New Paradigm Of Sword

When ink roars past, floods subside
And swells the nebula of law.
Behold the thinness of malign
That harnesses your jewel of pride.

The time, the moment, the second
You write off the minutes of prowess,
Nation will rise escorted by remains of justness.

Those irked by athirst orison you miss
When hell freezes over, will suck dry
And shun the convoys of sly.

The pen is new paradigm of sword,
The successor of war, as it cries halt
To the whole lot on fault.

# 19. Beyond Their Lies

Look upon the vicissitude of it's fortune
Don't let their garbs jewel mirages on it's beauty
See through every window of flaming house
And write down what you see beyond their lies

Go on shanks' mare on the highest hill unnamed
And cry of famished, crispy lipped to the norns
Listen to the silent echoes of your voice
And write down what you hear beyond their lies

Far in the dark in those cursed woods of dystopia
They are boundlessly abysmal, take up your abode there,
In all of it you eat happens to be the tang of blood
Taste it, and write down what you feel beyond their lies

Soon, they will be here in your caravans
Of leftover scruples, and you as I suspect
Could not eschew, hold the pen one last time
And write down everything what you know beyond their lies

# 20. The Muharram Rivers

Cobwebs tied up in the olfactory caves,
Wet deserts of watch globes
And in unheedful lobes
Cobwebs tied up in blithe and graves.

And no factor of awareness
Is pristine among us.
In the country, we are dark bright,
Snowdrop, of no white.

Our threads__weave hell for us__
Of courage but strengthless.
O they who could promise us the end,
Row our ark and suspend

The Muharram rivers to revive,
Are stained with perjury, and in gyve
Of hush money, that devoured them
Together with the cry of freedom.

.

.

.

Wake up O wake up ! and discord
The follow suit, for those who clawed
The dwelling peace are to each of us
And each of us measure out injustice.

# 21. Death Shouldn't Be Mourned

The mimic winds of shores
Eager to touch the fire
Of fulgent chinars in nishat
And whisper in their ears

The sighs of those drowned
For the aura of Eden's Dal.
And say, do not grieve,
Our death shouldn't be mourned.

Be proud, that we battled
Against the gliding streams.
When the seas obeyed
Their mischief and faded.

For it's oily mångata to shine
We kindled our soul orchids
And turned to pain, bestowed on you
The Kashmir of thine.

# About The Author

IRSHAD MUSHTAQ, Co-author of several books hails from Baramulla district of Kashmir. He is pursuing bachelors degree in GDC Baramulla. It's Irshad's reticent disposition that urged his paper to receive ink deals of his Pen. An admirer of Dervish's nerve, he has always wished to write like him and pony up a bit in service of his own Nation.

He feels himself so attracted towards the world of poetry and Novels. He uses writing as the tool to combat the curbs put forth by the world. Besides poetry, he is working on a novel as well that would be published soon. Save for literary interest, Irshad has a very deep liking for sports too. He feeds his addiction to it by watching football in evening.

Keep in touch with Irshad Mushtaq via:

Email: irshadtantray73@gmail.com

Ig: irrshadmushtaq

9 798887 337432

Printed by Libri Plureos GmbH in Hamburg,
Germany